The Thriving Caregiver Guided Journal

THIS JOURNAL BELONGS TO:

_____

PHONE: _____

EMAIL _____

Copyright © 2024

Designed by Carolyn Wheeler and
Joanna Andrick
Publisher: Meaningful Thoughts, LLC
ISBN: 978-0-9976764-8-8
Publication: 2024
Edition: 1
Printed in the USA

All rights reserved. No part of this book may be reproduced, distributed, or transmitted in any form or by any means without the prior written permission of the publisher, except for brief quotations used in reviews or critiques.

Daisy's Place™ The Thriving Caregiver™ Thriving Caregiver™ Caregivers helping caregivers™
The heart of our community.

For More Thriving Caregiver™ Resources Go To
ThrivingCaregiver.com

Welcome to The Thriving Caregiver's Guided Journal,

a space created with you in mind.

Caregiving asks so much of you, your time, your energy, your heart. This journal is here to offer something in return: a quiet place to reflect, breathe, and care for your inner world.

Within these pages, you'll find thoughtful prompts to help you name your feelings, celebrate your growth, and stay rooted in gratitude. Use it to process what's heavy, to record what's good, and to remember you are not alone in this journey. Whether you're writing from a place of strength or from sheer exhaustion, may these pages meet you with grace and gentleness.

"And let the peace of God rule in your hearts, to which also you were called in one body; and be thankful." Colossians 3:15 (NKJV)

With love,
Carolyn

For more encouragement, tools, and support created just for caregivers, explore the full collection, including The Thriving Caregiver book, planner, blank journal, and other caregiver resources.
www.ThrivingCaregiver.com

Three moments of joy that comfort me.

Two blessings I am thankful for today.

One challenge I've overcome and what it taught me.

Three acts of kindness I've experienced or shared.

Two ways I can prioritize self-care today.

One thing I accomplished today and feel proud of.

Three people who make my life brighter.

Two dreams I want to pursue and why they matter.

One unexpected blessing I've received recently.

Three things that bring me peace in stressful moments.

Two things I can let go of to feel more free.

One way I've grown in the past month.

Three places where I feel most at ease.

Two memories that always make me smile.

Three things I love about myself.

Two strengths I've relied on during hard times.

One lesson I've learned from a recent challenge.

Three small victories I've achieved lately.

Two things I'm most looking forward to.

One person I'm grateful for and why.

Three words that describe how I feel today.

Two ways I can create calm in my day.

Three things that inspire me to keep going.

Two habits I want to build for a better life.

One quote or scripture that resonates with me today.

Three things I've learned from caregiving.

Two ways I've seen resilience in myself.

One thing I've done recently to bring joy to someone else.

Three traits I admire in others and strive for myself.

Two hobbies or activities that relax me.

One thing I've learned from failure.

Three simple pleasures I treasure daily.

Two ways I can be more present in my life.

One area where I'd like to improve and how I can start.

Three things I've done this year that I'm proud of.

Two skills I've developed through caregiving.

One act of self-love I can do today.

Three qualities that make me unique.

Two moments when I've felt closest to God.

One way I've helped someone recently.

Three things I'm learning to appreciate about myself.

Two moments of laughter I've enjoyed this week.

One unexpected joy I've experienced this year.

Three relationships I'm thankful for and why.

One way I've prioritized myself recently.

Two blessings I often overlook but am grateful for.

One way I can bring more balance into my life.

Three things that make me feel hopeful about the future.

Two moments where I felt truly seen and valued.

Two things I want to celebrate about myself today.

www.ingramcontent.com/pod-product-compliance
Lightning Source LLC
Chambersburg PA
CBHW052212090526
44584CB00019BA/3055